GOLDEN RULES

Please follow these three rules

Students should:

 Always SING the melody as they PLAY, using the animal names (for example "Dog, Bird, Goose ...")

 COUNT aloud during the RHYTHM exercises, clapping, tapping, or playing notes chosen by the teacher

 NEVER tap or play FASTER than one beat a second

THE KEYBOARD

Rhythm Exercises 1

a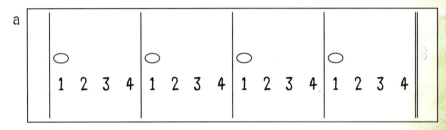

b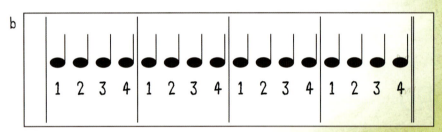

c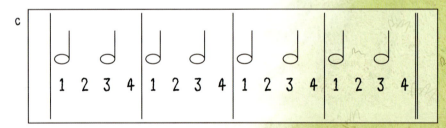

Count evenly and slowly as you clap or tap these rhythms.
It may help if you march around the room, in the garden
or in the playground, when you count and clap.

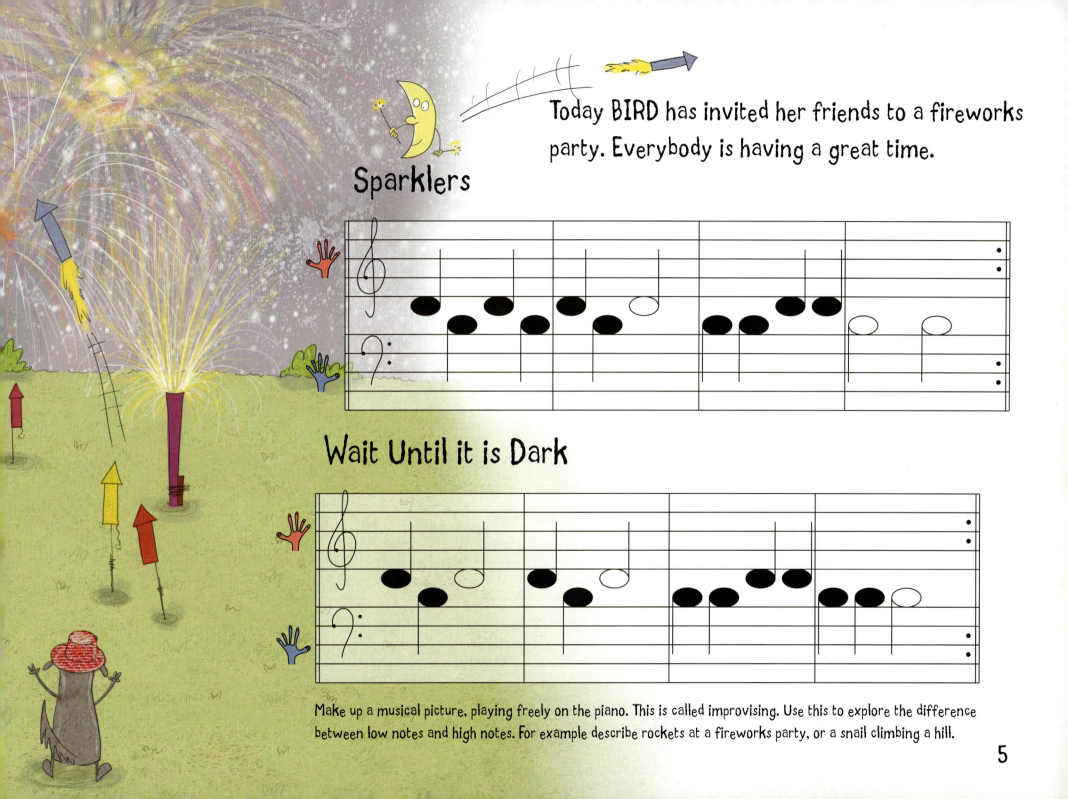

In the Bush

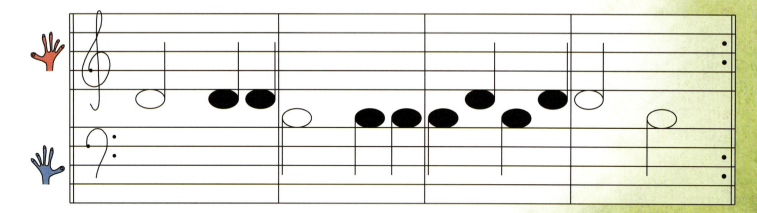

Cotton Flower

Make up a short melody using DOGs and BIRDs. If you have a set of Animal Tiles and Coloured Staves you can use those. Play your melody everywhere on the piano, singing at the most comfortable pitch as you play.

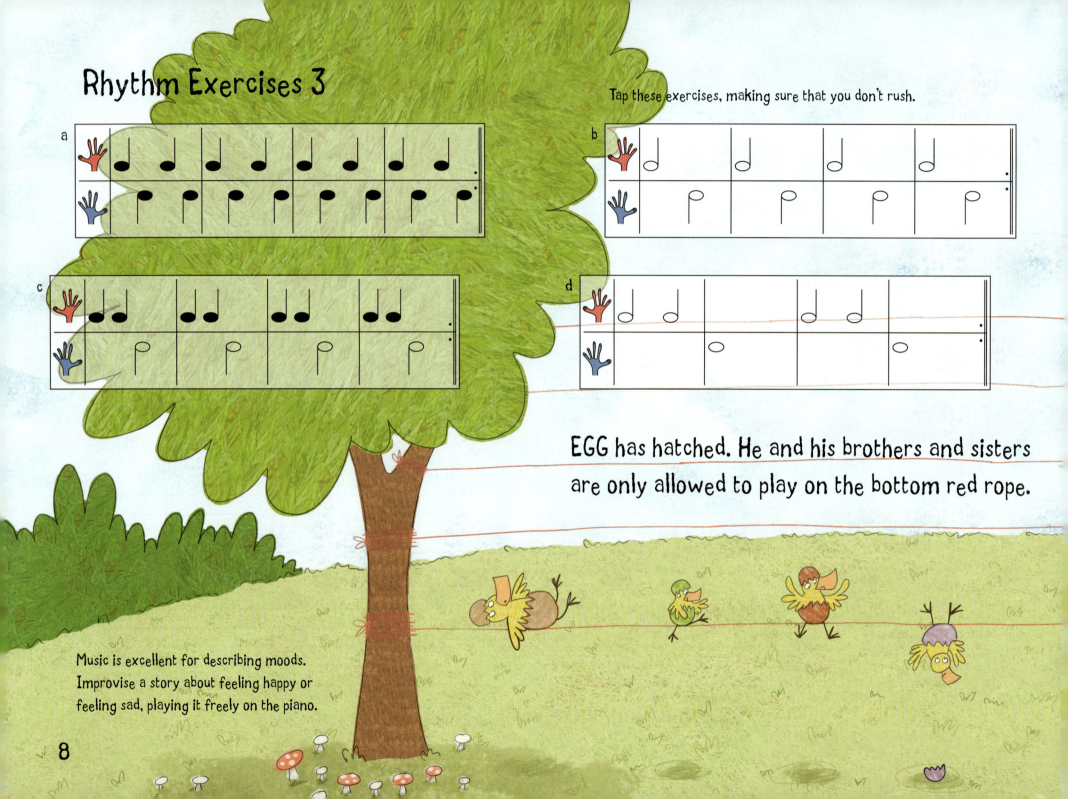

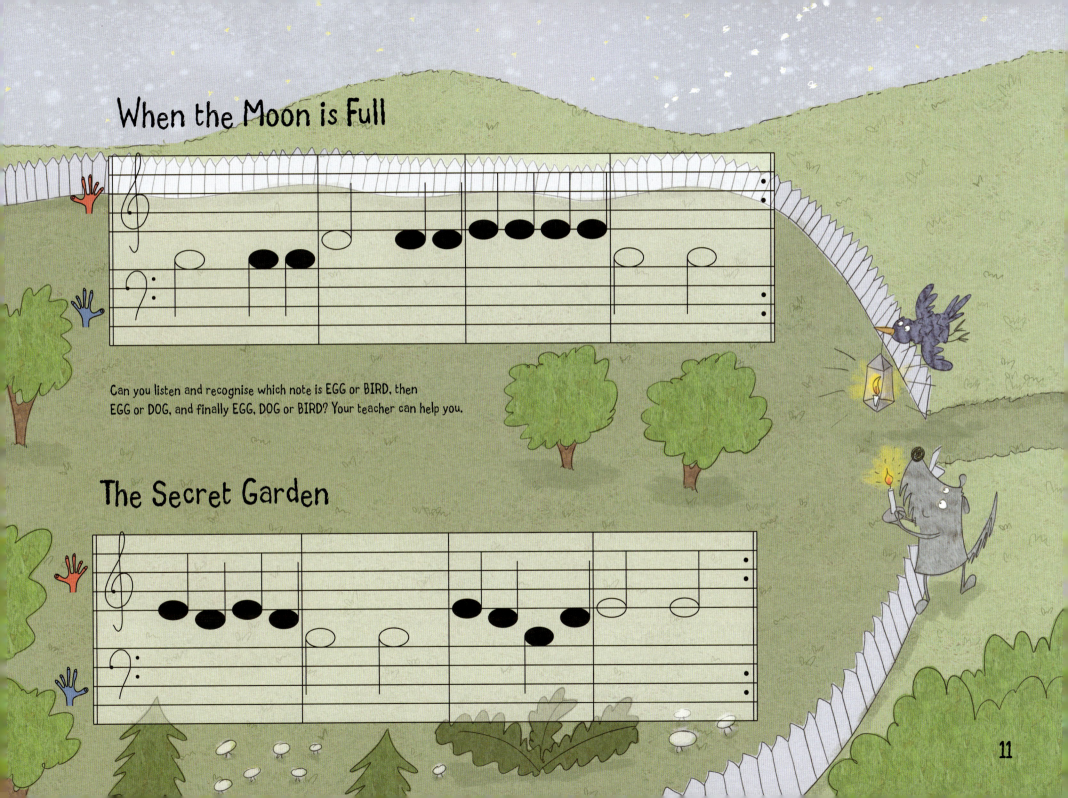

Rhythm Exercises 4

a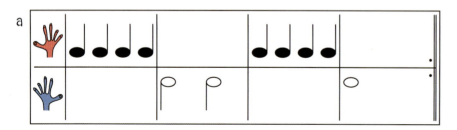

b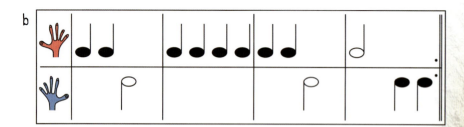

c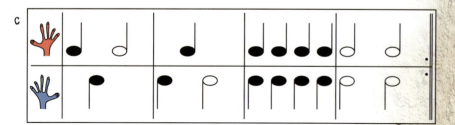

d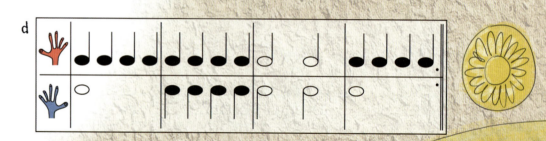

If exercise 4d is too hard then try tapping the right (RED) hand part only, with your teacher tapping the left (BLUE) hand part. Then swap hands with your teacher. Finally tap the rhythm exercise on your own.

The Egg Rock tells DOG and BIRD to head for the Bazaar in Morocco, where they will find a magic carpet.

Golden Rings

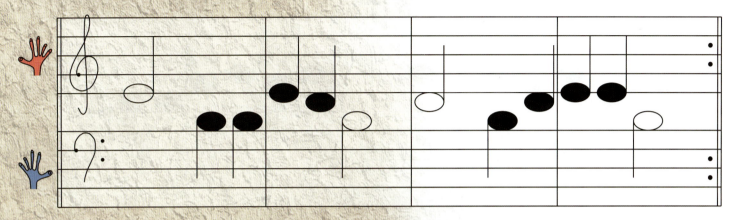

Rug from Morocco

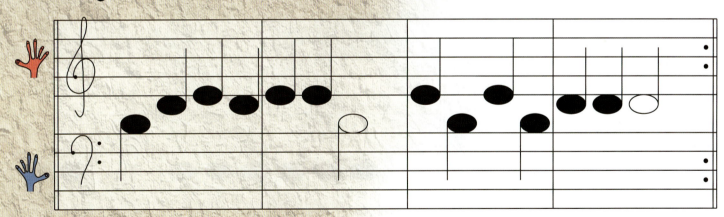

Play a copying game with your teacher. Form musical phrases using EGG, DOG and BIRD with a maximum of 4 to 6 notes, and copy each other's phrases. Play detached notes from the shoulder, using the whole arm.

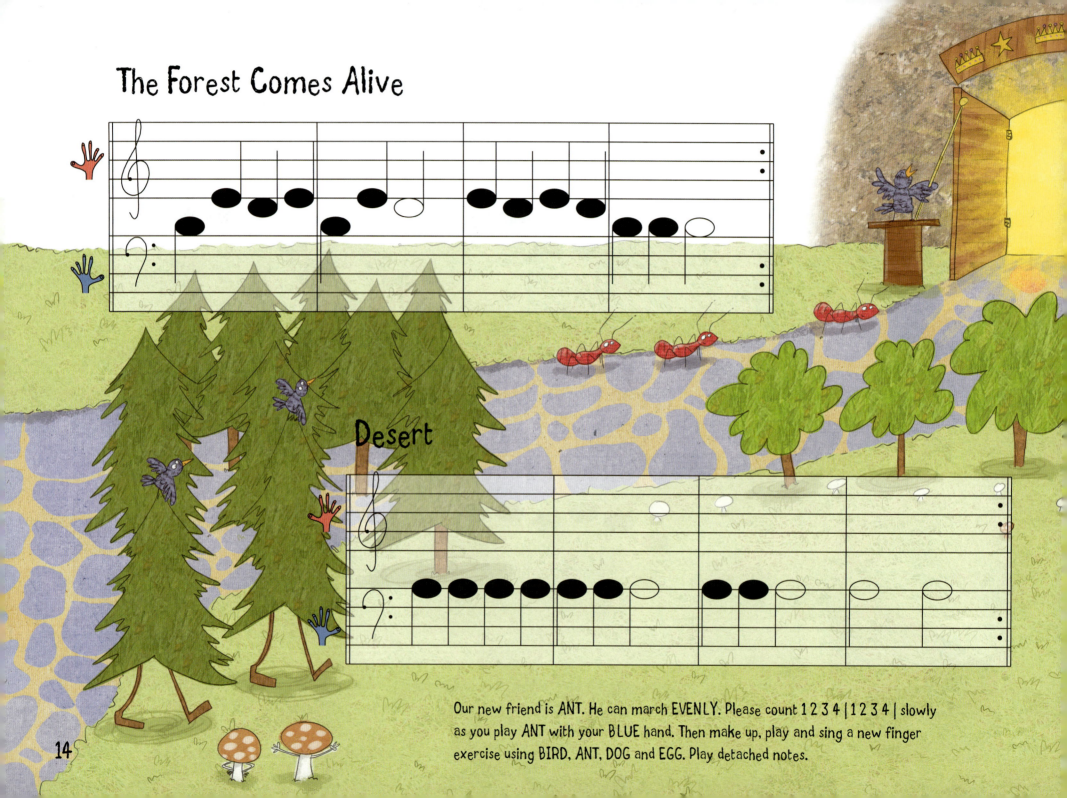

Rhythm Exercises 5

If it is difficult to hold down one hand for four beats,
try learning these exercises practising one bar at a time.

Once you have learnt to play and sing "Watch the Milky Way", then try to play it from memory.

Watch the Milky Way

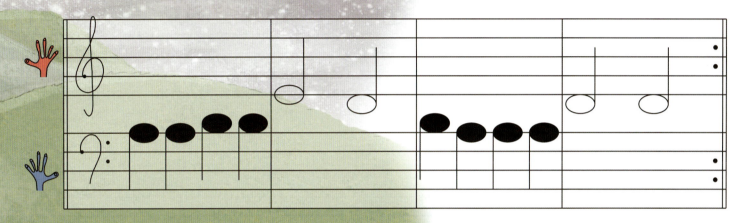

Great Smoky Mountain

Spring has arrived. It is a lovely evening, and the friends go out together to watch the stars.

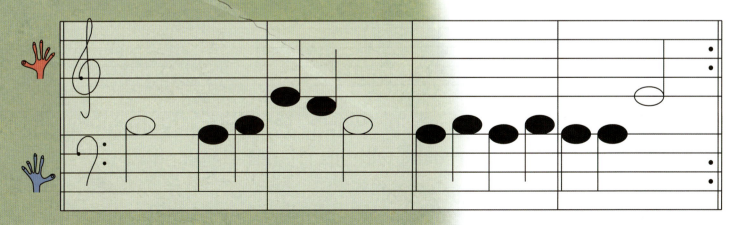

17

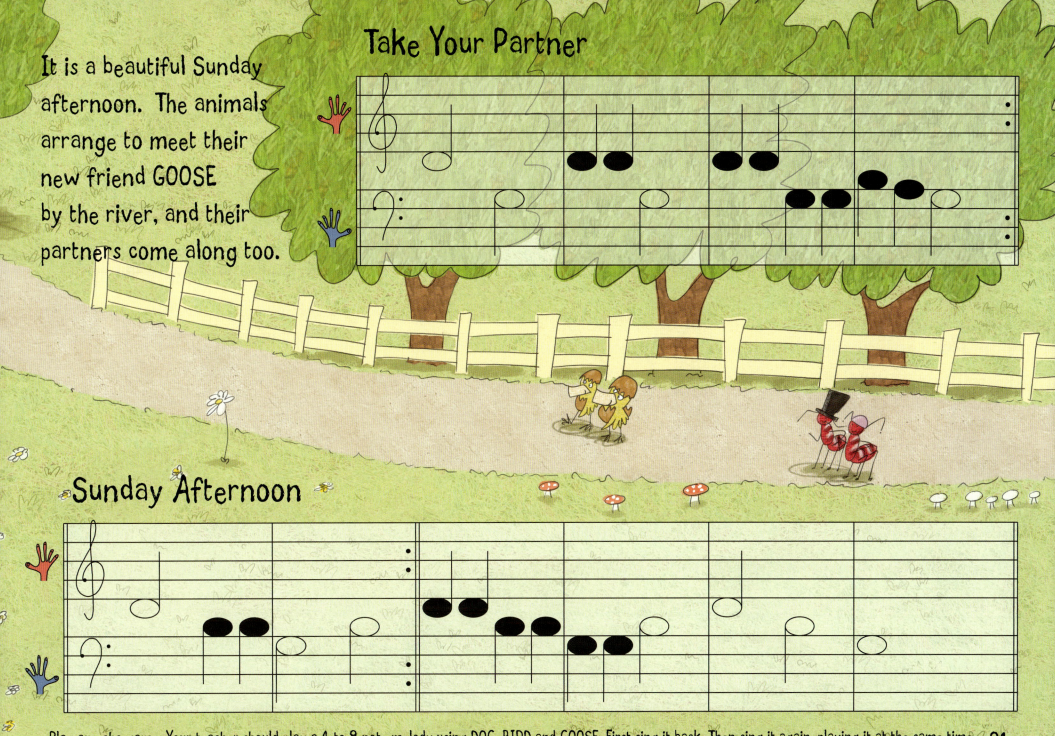

It is a beautiful Sunday afternoon. The animals arrange to meet their new friend GOOSE by the river, and their partners come along too.

Take Your Partner

Sunday Afternoon

Play an echo game. Your teacher should play a 4 to 8 note melody using DOG, BIRD and GOOSE. First sing it back. Then sing it again, playing it at the same time.

Rhythm Exercises 7

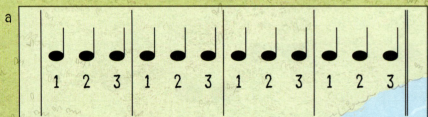

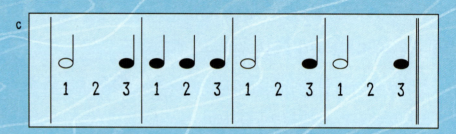

With 3 beats in a bar (box) counting can easily become uneven. Make sure that the 3rd beat is not too long. If you count slowly for the 1st and 2nd beats, then probably the 3rd beat will be correct. "Waltz" and clap 1 2 3 | 1 2 3 |.

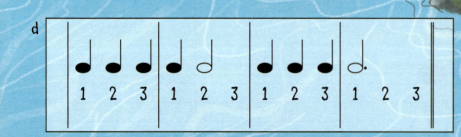

The next day the river is flowing very fast as the snow melts in the mountains. Everybody finds it difficult to cross over to the other side.

Skipping Stones

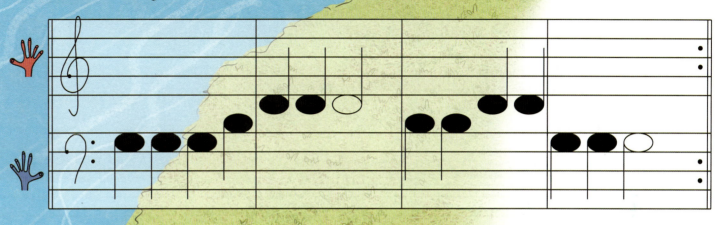

Wheelbarrow

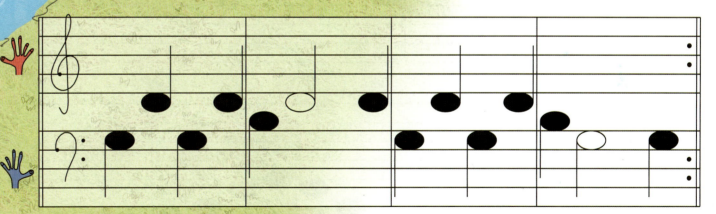

A STEP is the interval between two notes next to each other, for example ANT to BIRD or DOG to EGG. GOOSE to BIRD, and BIRD to DOG are SKIPs. In a SKIP the next door animal is missed out. Learn to play STEP UP, STEP DOWN, SKIP UP and SKIP DOWN. Your teacher will help you.

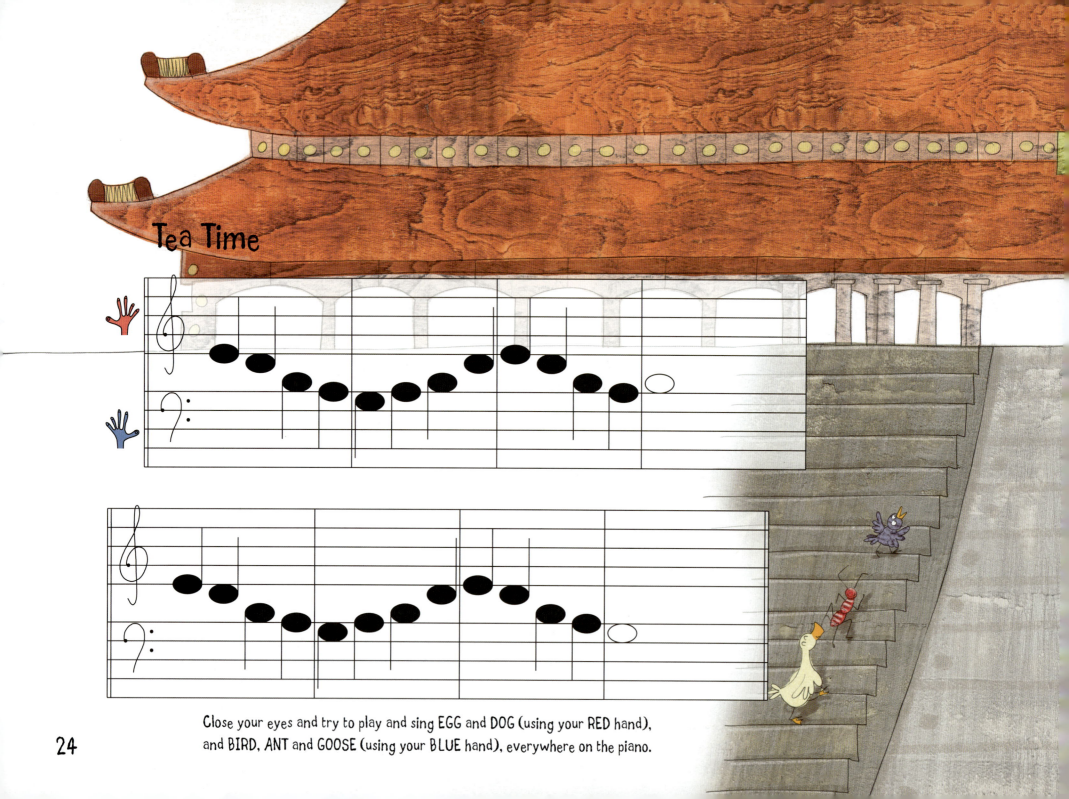

Chinese Pagoda

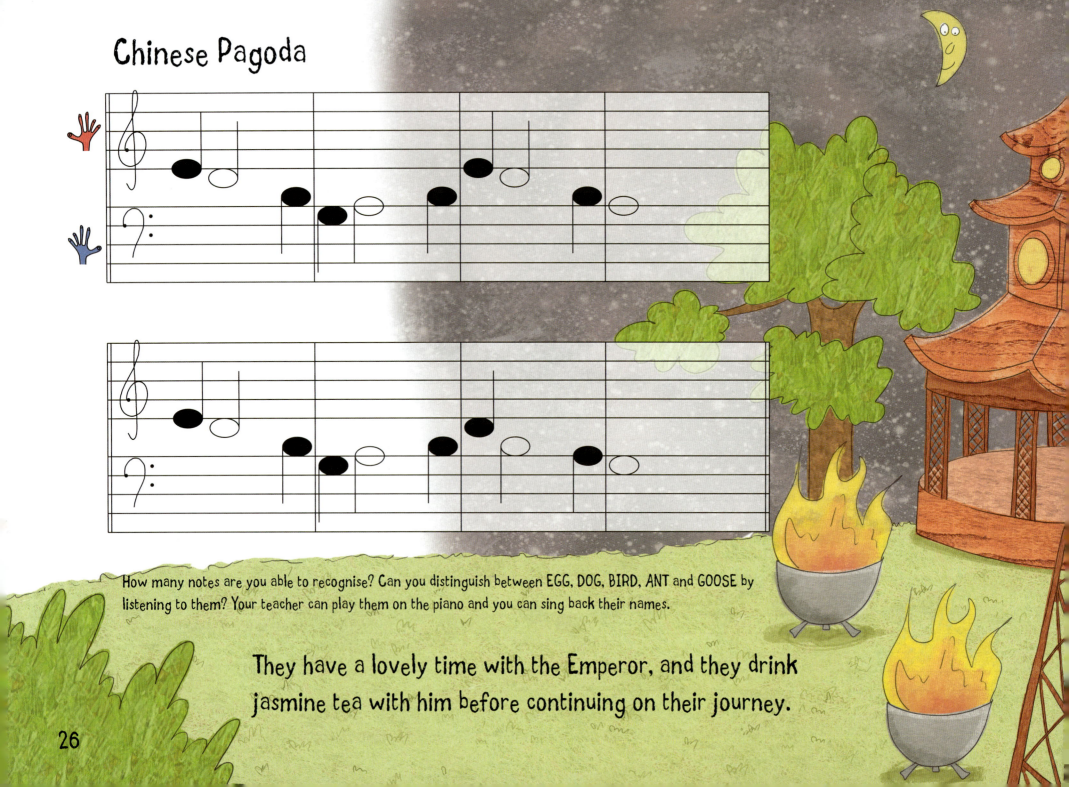

How many notes are you able to recognise? Can you distinguish between EGG, DOG, BIRD, ANT and GOOSE by listening to them? Your teacher can play them on the piano and you can sing back their names.

They have a lovely time with the Emperor, and they drink jasmine tea with him before continuing on their journey.

Rhythm Exercises 8

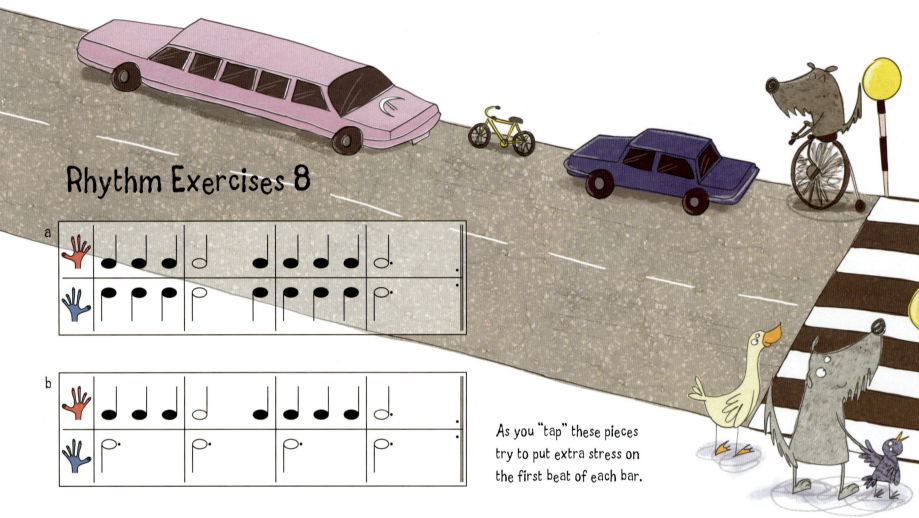

As you "tap" these pieces try to put extra stress on the first beat of each bar.

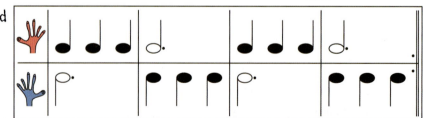

As they go to the airport in Beijing the friends get held up in a traffic jam.

Hands Together

Traffic Jam

Make up a finger exercise in two parts. Start by holding down EGG or DOG with the right hand and then add a melody with the left hand using BIRD and GOOSE.

29

Jack and His Men

32 If you know this piece well, you can try to play the RED hand part only and sing the BLUE hand part at the same time, using the animal names.

Rhythm Exercises 9

a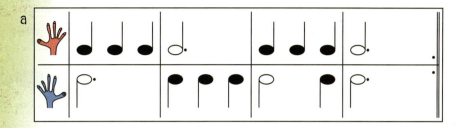

b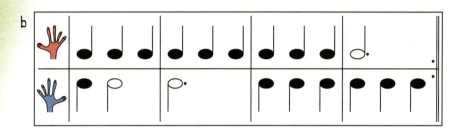

c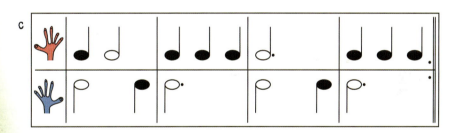

d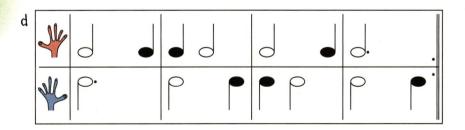

Make up your own melody using the notes from "Jack and his Men". You can use the Animal Tiles and Coloured Staves for this.

While the animals are away on their travels, Jack the Ant and his workers are building a house for their new neighbour.

33

Rhythm Exercises 10

a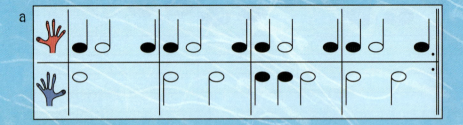

b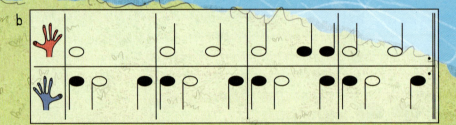

c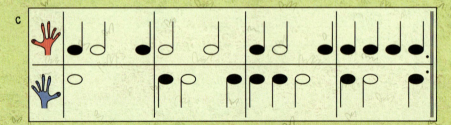

d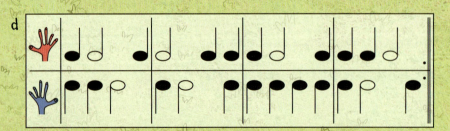

The animals must find one more friend to complete their team. They decide to float down the river in search of a new member.

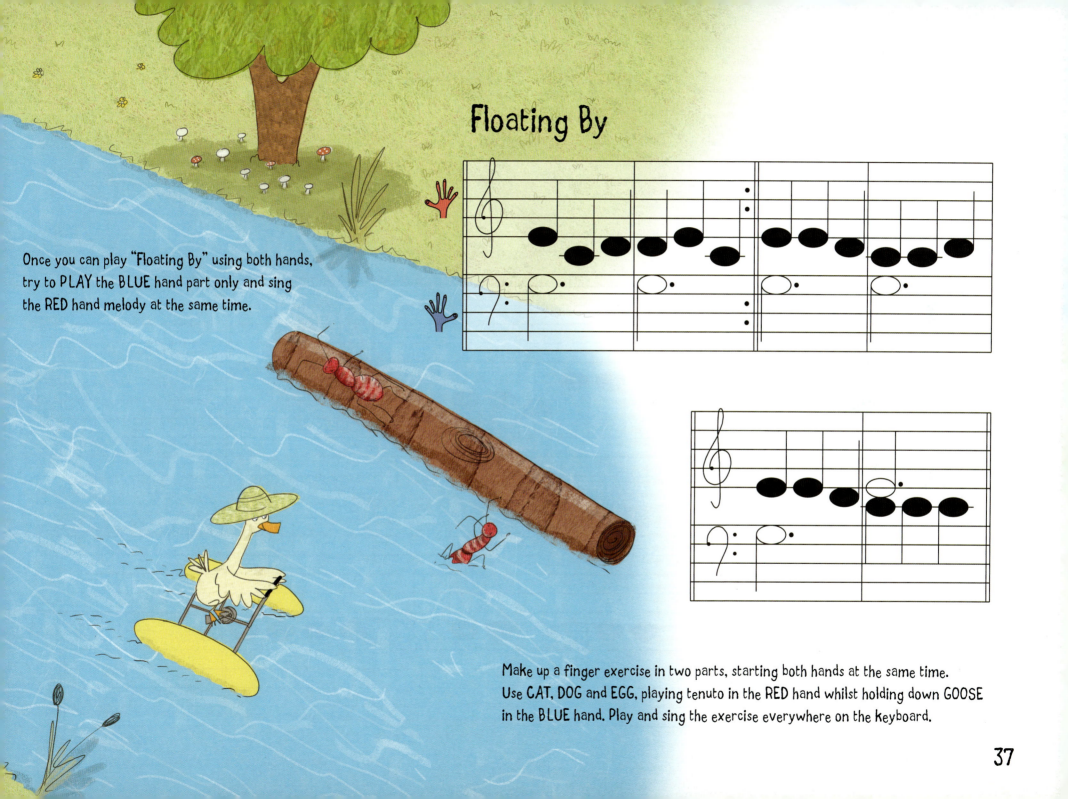

Old MacDonald just happens to have a prize singing fish. "I am sure she would love to join your group", he says. So FISH leaves with the others to become the final member of the team of musical animals.

Aquarium

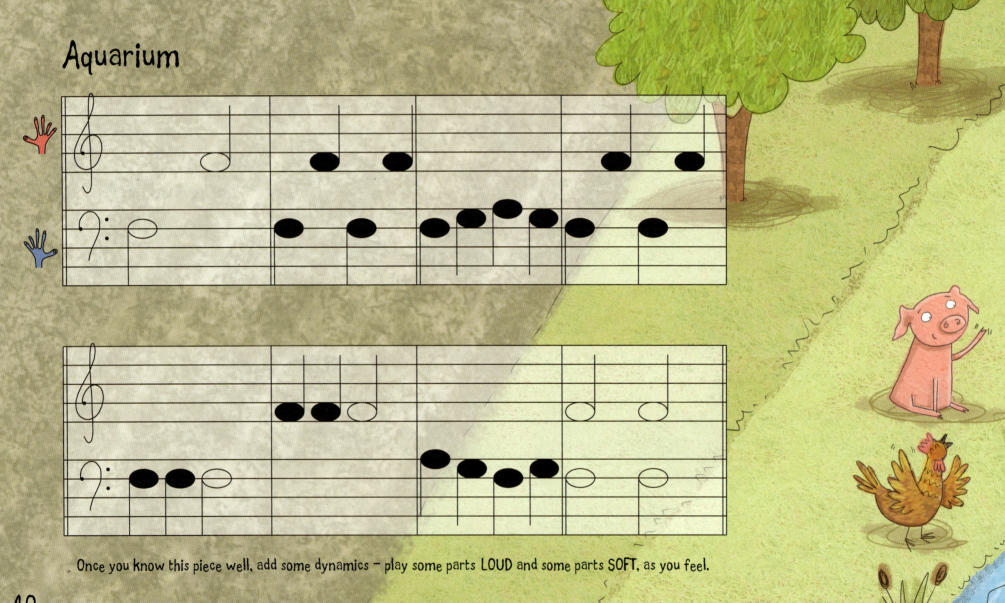

Once you know this piece well, add some dynamics – play some parts LOUD and some parts SOFT, as you feel.

Wishing Well

Once you know "Wishing Well", try to play the RED part only and sing the BLUE hand melody at the same time, using the animal names.

All the animals visit the Wishing Well to ask for Christmas presents, before they go carol singing.

42

All Over the Universe

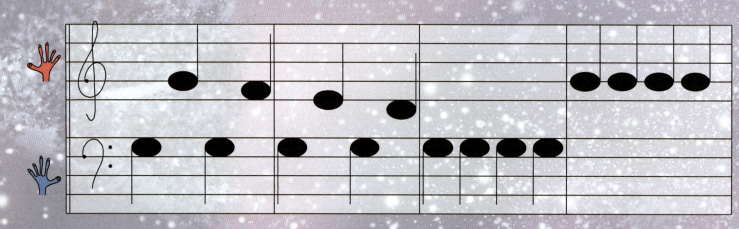

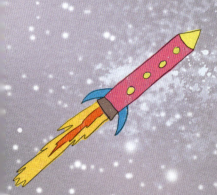

Just as the animals are off exploring the universe, you are now ready to carry on with your exploration of the piano.

The Basic Elements of the Dogs and Birds Approach

A whole range of musical exercises and games should be used, in addition to playing the musical pieces and "tapping" the rhythm exercises, as you work through Dogs and Birds. They add variety to the lessons and practice, and help develop the musical awareness of the child. Most pages of this book include suggestions for performing these additional musical activities, which are outlined below. Please feel free to make up similar games and exercises based on those described here. Further details can be found in the Notes to Book 1 for Parents and Teachers, which also contains a set of lesson plans. It is available from www.dogsandbirds.co.uk.

Videos – Examples of the various activities described below can be seen on the Dogs and Birds Piano Method YouTube channel at www.youtube.com/user/elzalusher.

The Importance of Daily Practice – At this stage it is much more important to practise for a short time each day, rather than a longer period less frequently. Ask the child to practise for 5 minutes every day (both singing and playing the pieces). The practice should be varied. Each day the child should play and sing two pieces and perform two of the other activities. You will see rapid progress and the child's concentration span will increase tremendously.

Length of Lessons – A typical lesson time is 30 minutes. Each lesson should be broken up into smaller parts. It should contain around 5 or 6 of the musical activities. This will allow the child to concentrate for a short time on each of the elements. Work at the child's own pace and do not force anything – the lessons should always be fun.

The Small Animal Tiles and Coloured Staves – Use of the tiles and staves is highly recommended as an integral part of the Dogs and Birds approach. They form a "board game" that can be used in almost all of the musical exercises and games. Children love playing with the 56 different animals, and playing the board game truly enhances the learning process.

Use of the Blank Notes Edition – The main difference between the blank and animal books is that animal symbols are not printed in the notes in the blank notes edition. Both books should be used in the same way, with the child always singing the animal names. The ultimate aim is for children to be able to read without the use of the animal symbols. Some children enjoy the challenge of this and use the blank book from the start. Others start using the blank book after they have gained confidence in playing from the animal book. The two editions can also be used in parallel. You can put both books on the piano and ask the child to play from the blank book, with the animal book there as a "safety net". Use of the tiles and staves helps enormously with the transition from animal to blank notation.

The Use of Toys – Ask the children to involve a favourite toy in their lessons or practice. It can be a finger puppet or cuddly toy. These toys can visit the various animals, play notes on the keyboard, help with tapping, and stimulate the child's imagination. Please do not underestimate the importance of games and toys in the learning process.

A Note on Singing – Singing is a vitally important aspect of the Dogs and Birds approach. It helps to develop musicality and to train the child's inner-ear. Singing teaches phrasing musical sentences, and shaping melodies naturally, just as reading aloud improves speech. Singing is the best way to improve the ear, and a better ear will produce better music. It is essential that the child always sings the animal names whilst playing. You should encourage this by singing along as well. Some children find singing difficult initially. In these cases they should say the names as they play. With time and practice they will eventually be able to sing.

A Note on Fingering and Technique – The most appropriate fingering will depend on the child, since the physical development of very young children is different in each case. For this reason finger numbers are not used in Book 1 – they are introduced at the start of Book 2. Children should play from the shoulder, with each note detached, using the whole arm, hands and fingers as one unit. It is very important for future development of technique that the child learns to play a detached tenuto (separated notes) before trying to play legato (smoothly). Therefore, throughout Book 1 students should always play tenuto. By the end of Book 1 students in general should be able to play using first (thumb), second (index) and third (middle) fingers in both hands, using a correct hand position with curved fingers. Use of the fourth and fifth fingers is not recommended, unless the child is ready. It is advisable to start this book using the right (red) hand thumb for Dog and the left (blue) hand thumb for Bird. However if the child is younger than 3 it might be better to use the index fingers.

Sung Finger Exercises – Every lesson try to make up a bar or two-bar phrase based on the pieces from the lesson. You should ask the child to play it at every octave on the piano or keyboard, whilst singing the animal names. Children should always sing at the most comfortable pitch, which will probably be the one closest to middle C. Very young children should perform these exercises standing at the piano and should walk to the left and right in order to reach the notes. As well as preparing the child for playing the pieces, these little studies will help with ear-training and singing, strengthen the fingers, introduce the geography of the keyboard, and prepare for improvisation and composition.

Sight-Singing – Before you begin to play a piece you should sing the melody together with the child using the animal names. For example, before starting to play "Open Gate" on page 15 you should first play and sing "ANT, BIRD, DOG, EGG" a couple of times. Then sing the piece with the child before playing it. For very young children it will help if you point out each note on the musical score using your fingers as you sing it. Use your right hand index finger for notes in the treble clef and your left hand index finger for bass clef notes. For pieces that are played hands together (first met on page 29) you should sing the melody before playing.

Rhythm Exercises – These are dispersed throughout the book. You should always COUNT as you tap the rhythm exercises. An excellent way to "tap", which children enjoy, is for them to play many notes at once on the keyboard using their palms. Play from the shoulders using a relaxed arm. You can also use a table top for tapping. It is quite common for very young children (under five years old) to find the rhythm exercises harder than the musical pieces, but please do not neglect them. They are extremely important in providing a strong foundation for feeling the beat, for helping the child to learn to count out loud, and ultimately with helping to play hands together. Very young children often struggle with coordination in these exercises, and many have difficulty distinguishing between left and right. You can mark the child's right and left hands red and blue with marker pens, or use coloured rubber bands or ribbons around the child's wrists to help identify the hands.

Improvisation – This gives a lot of freedom to children, which is why they enjoy it very much. Usually the student and teacher make up a story together. This story could be about a train – it approaches the station, stops, allows people get on and off, blows its whistle, and leaves the station. Another idea is to describe animals – a snake climbs up to the top of a tree to catch a singing bird. Or improvise a story about being in the playground when it starts to rain and a storm breaks out. Children can use their palms, fists, forearms, the backs of their hands, or any of their fingers to play notes as they "paint" these stories. Add as much dynamics and expression as possible.

Learning the Musical Pieces – When the child learns the pieces you should first talk about the titles and the story. Then sight-sing the melody as described earlier. Finally play the piece. Make sure the child always sings the animal names whilst playing, and doesn't play too fast.

A Listening Game – When you are learning to play any instrument it is important to learn to use your ear, not just your eyes, hands, body and mind. Hence this activity is very beneficial, especially later on. It will help children to improve their ear day by day. First they should learn to identify two different notes. Play and sing DOG and BIRD on the piano and ask the child to try to recognise them, singing them back. It helps if you point to an image of a DOG and BIRD as you play. You can, for example, use the animal tiles for this. As you progress through Book 1 you should add more animals as the child encounters them.

An Echo Game – This is a more complex version of the listening game. Play a short musical phrase using notes the child knows and ask him or her to sing it back. The child should point out where the appropriate animals sit on the staves (either with a stick or pencil) whilst singing their names.

A Copying Game – With this exercise the child will learn to play a short melody as an echo on the keyboard. Play a short melody using, for example, the notes in the piece that the child is currently studying. Then ask the child to play the melody back to you, singing the animal names at the same time. First allow the child to see your hands as you play. With practice children will eventually be able to do this exercise without looking at your hands.

Composition – For very young children it is recommended to use the small animal tiles and coloured staves for this exercise. The idea is to make up a short melody using the notes they know. They can place a series of various animal notes on their correct positions on the staves using Blu-Tack (or an equivalent adhesive putty). They can then place the staves onto the piano in place of a musical score and play their composition. Older children can write their compositions directly into a manuscript book. In general the compositions should be similar to the pieces the child is learning in the lesson.

Drawing – It is always important to stimulate the child's imagination. Please encourage your child or students to draw images inspired by the musical pieces or their improvisations, and bring them to you when you have a lesson.

Using String or Masking Tape to Represent Staves – It is always good for a child to stand up away from the piano during a lesson. Place a line of masking tape on the floor, or tape down some string. Call the line the ANT's line. Play ANTs and ask the child to walk along the line. The child should step "above" the line if you play a BIRD and step "below" it if you play a GOOSE. You can repeat this game using different notes. You can add more lines to make a full stave. Very small children can play this game by walking on the large set of staves.

The Dogs and Birds method, with its strong emphasis on singing, has its roots in the approach of Hungarian music educator Zoltán Kodály.

Notes for Parents

Musical Notation and Symbols

- In music it is necessary to symbolize both the length of a note (how long or short it is) and its pitch (how high or low it is). The notes on a piano keyboard are grouped together, with 12 pitches (seven white keys and five black keys) in each group. A note of a certain pitch is given a name. In this book only white notes of the keyboard are used. These notes